Nested Loops Demystified:

Revealing the Art of Multilevel Communication and Unconscious Instillation in NLP

MATT CAULFIELD

Copyright © 2013 Matt Caulfield

Matt Caulfield is hereby identified as author of this work in accordance with section 77 of the Copyright, Designs and Patents Act.

The author has asserted his moral rights.

ISBN: 1491095954
ISBN-13: 9781491095959

DEDICATION

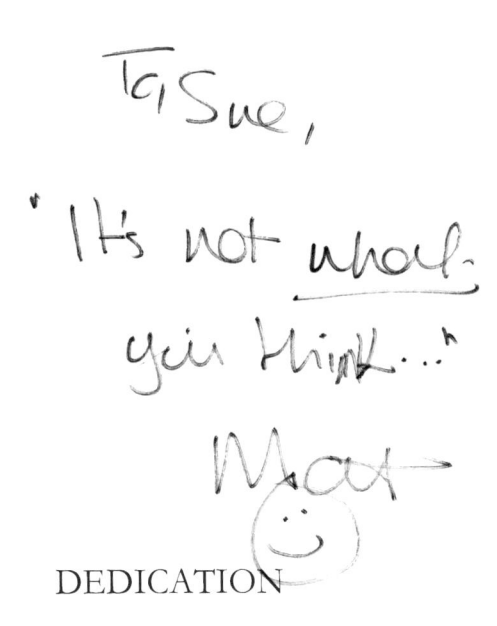

For my wife Jen, who puts up with me!
And to everyone who has inspired and supported me (you know who you are).

CONTENTS

	Acknowledgments	i
	About The Author	ii
	Note To The Text	iii
PART 1	BEFORE WE BEGIN	1
PART 2	SOME THINGS YOU NEED TO KNOW BEFORE USING NESTED LOOPS	8
PART 3	WHAT NESTED LOOPS AREN'T	17
PART 4	WHAT NESTED LOOPS ARE	27
PART 5	HOW TO DESIGN NESTED LOOPS	38
PART 6	GOING DEEPER – MULTIPLE LOOPS	61
PART 7	GOING EVEN DEEPER – GETTING CREATIVE	67
PART 8	WHAT NEXT	72

ACKNOWLEDGMENTS

A teacher is a conduit between the information and the student. A teacher's job is to impart the information in a way that is easily learned.

So to begin I would like to acknowledge and thank those that helped train and inspire me to become a good teacher; Richard Bandler, Michael Breen, Bob Spour and Phil Seaton.

I would have nothing to teach if it had not been for the extraordinary innovators of NLP; Richard Bandler and John Grinder the two co-founders, as well as those I have trained with through the years and given me information to impart, especially Michael Breen, Charles Faulkner, John La Valle and Paul McKenna.

ABOUT THE AUTHOR

Matt Caulfield is an internationally recognized coach and trainer. He utilizes NLP and other related tools to help people improve their learning, critical thinking and communication skills. As he says, *"In an increasingly competitive, fast moving and complicated world, it is the quality of thinking that gives the edge. The clearer and better you think, the smarter and faster you go."*

To learn more visit his website www.mattcaulfield.co.uk where he writes a regular blog. It's not WHAT you think...

IMPORTANT NOTES TO THE TEXT:

1) This book assumes a basic and general understanding of NLP before you begin.

2) For the sake of brevity and ease of reading/use I make several assumptions and claims without expressly stating the evidence for that claim or assumption. This book is not designed to be a treatise *about* Nested Loops, but a manual about *how* to put them into action.

2) I use the term "story" in it's broadest possible context. The story could be a metaphor, it could be a joke or comical story, it could be a specific example, an anecdote, a news story, something that you have just made up to demonstrate a point, a generally accepted truism, etc.

3) For ease of example, in the text I talk about using Nested Loops in a group setting, and refer to "students" rather than the "client" etc. This does not mean that Nested Loops can only be used in a group setting. With a bit of imagination and adaption you can use Nested Loops within trance-work, or other one to one work (coaching for example) as well as in meetings, casual environments and anywhere you want to impart information in an engaging and compelling manner.

NESTED LOOPS DEMYSTIFIED

PART 1

BEFORE WE BEGIN

Introduction

Nested Loops and "unconscious instillation" have grown to almost mythical status in NLP.

People act as if they are some holy grail of persuasion and influence, but very few people in NLP know what they actually are, let alone how to use them correctly. A lot of NLPers pay lip service to the unconscious and unconscious instillation in training and therapy, but very few actually do it. Or they don't do it very well. I have seen very experienced and well-respected NLP trainers make a total mess of using and explaining Nested Loops (every clip I have seen on YouTube up to the time of writing that attempts to explain Nested Loops gets it wrong).

In reality, Nested Loops are very simple. This simplicity is deceptive, because Nested Loops are powerful; this is why Richard Bandler and his trainers can pack so much information into a 7-day training, information that it takes other people much longer to teach.

It also doesn't mean they are easy to master. One of the reasons that Nested Loops may be considered an "advanced" NLP skill is because you have to understand and be competent with quite a few other pieces of NLP methodology to use them.

One of the reasons Nested Loops have become almost mythical and are so often so badly understood, or implement, or confused with other concepts is there has been very little documentation available to help people learn and understand them. The aim of this book is to cut through the myths and misunderstandings to give you a simple way to start using Nested Loops and multilevel communication straight away. I have taken a lot of time and effort researching and practicing Nested Loops and now present my findings to you in the hope that they can teach you the skills and ability to use them yourself.

A Shaggy Dog Story?

I remember precisely where I was the first time I heard Richard Bandler.

Although I didn't know it at the time it was the start of an adventure that would continue to this day, that would lead to revelation, frustration, cul-de-sacs, backtracking and huge loops back on myself, but it would never be boring!

I was sitting in the car of my Thai Boxing instructor driving to the Friday night class at the University of Birmingham. The classes were always huge and it took a number of instructors (myself included) to be able to manage the class effectively. It was autumn, the light was just starting to fade and the leaves on the trees starting to turn brown. Autumn is one of my favorite seasons (along with winter, spring and summer) the change it brings always makes it seem magic(k)al and many new ventures, interests and adventures seem to start in autumn for me.

This particular autumn I was 22, I had always had an enquiring mind and had been having a "what is life all about?" existential crisis for as long as I could remember. I had a thirst for knowledge, more than that, a thirst for practical, visceral experience. I had learned that theories are all well and interesting, but you can't hang your coat on them (at the time I didn't realize that a "working theory" was as good as I would probably get).

I can't recall the tape-set (tapes! Remember them?!) that Bob had in the car, but I recall Richard telling an anecdote about being mugged and defending himself with a chocolate gun. Anyone that has heard Richard talk will know this is a usual type of story for him!

I remember thinking this doesn't sound like self help, it sounded like a stand up comedian.

He seemed to effortlessly weave one story into another and before I knew it I was transfixed. I knew there and then that I needed some of that!

Richard Bandler, through the years, has developed a unique and powerful way to get across vast amounts of information in a very condensed way, without the audience really having to work hard to learn the information presented.

In much the same way, my favorite teacher, Phil Seaton, who taught me A-level Biology, had this incredible knack of being able to just tell us stories in the lessons and it didn't feel like we had to work hard to learn anything. In fact it didn't feel like we were learning (in the slow, painful way I had come to understand the term) anything at all, just sitting there listening to Phil entertain us. He would set us homework at the end the class and I would think, "we never learned anything about that." But somehow, when I actually sat down to do it, the answers would pop into my head. Phil had snuck them in there during his story telling without me noticing.

In fact, all the great teachers I have experienced have had a way of making the subject come alive; of using stories and anecdotes to wrap up information in an easily understandable way.

A shaggy dog story is traditionally an extremely long-winded tale featuring many irrelevant tangents, off topic distractions and unnecessary details.

Told well they can hold people's attention and interest. Typical examples of Shaggy Dog Stories are Ronnie Corbett's monologues in the UK TV series the Two Ronnie's, the Lost TV series and some of the films of Guy Richie (particularly Snatch).

Richard Bandler, the co-creator of NLP is a master of using the structure of shaggy dog stories to embed, demonstrate and teach NLP skills, methodology and most importantly attitude.

Anyone can tell a long and rambling story, it is the structure and design of that story that makes it work. I have seen many people attempt to "model" Rich Bandler's delivery style, but they tend to miss the underlying structure and purpose and just go for the surface level. They just end up telling rambling stories.

Stories have always been used to teach. From the birth of civilization we have used stories to pass on knowledge or explain the world around us (modern scientific explanations are no less stories than the early creation myths. Science is just a better researched story...). It is why we are so transfixed by (good) storytellers and why being an effective storyteller is essential to being able to teach a subject effectively.

Nested Loops uses stories to create a powerful learning state within people and weave the learnings deep inside.

PART 2

SOME THINGS YOU NEED TO KNOW BEFORE USING NESTED LOOPS

Before We Begin (Again)

Nested Loops are what could be considered an "advanced" NLP tool. The reason for this is you need to understand and have a reasonable capability in a broad range of NLP methodology. I will refer to some of these in more detail than others depending on the relevance and importance to Nest Loops. If you are unsure of anything I mention I recommend you spend some time reviewing and revising it before you start planning your Nested Loops.

Before you can attempt to use Nested Loops specifically you need to be comfortable with the idea of:
- Well-formed Outcomes.
- State.
- The Strategy Model including the T.O.T.E
- The basic language patterns - The Meta Model and the Milton Model.

But even before that, we need to go way back to first principles and clarify some core concepts...

The Conscious and Unconscious Mind

The idea of the unconscious mind was first coined by the 18th century German philosopher Friedrich Schelling. It was introduced into English by the poet and essayist Samuel Taylor

Coleridge (it is interesting to note here, although not relevant to the topic, that humanities once again led science in our understanding of the human mind). The concept was developed and popularized by Sigmund Freud in the development of his psychoanalytic approaches.

And it is wrong.

Well, that is a bit unfair, maybe it is better to say it is often misunderstood.

Our mind cannot be split into a conscious and unconscious part. That false dichotomy is brought about by badly defined and explained categorization that has snuck into our collective understanding to the point that it is no longer really thought of and questioned.

In reality there is no such thing as an unconscious or conscious part of the mind, there are simply those processes going on that we are either consciously or not consciously aware of.

Conscious and Unconscious Awareness

It would be more accurate to use the terms conscious and unconscious 'awareness' rather than 'mind'. What really is going on is there are mental processes that are going on all the time. We can call some of these processes into conscious awareness; we can become aware of things we are thinking/doing and the reason for doing them. In fact the majority of psychological therapies from Freudian psychoanalysis to NLP rely on our ability to become consciously aware of our thoughts and behavior so we can change them. To split the mind up into a conscious and unconscious part presupposes there is a section we can never become aware of, which is not borne out by the evidence.

When we learn to do something really well, it tends to slip out of conscious awareness. How often do you have to really consciously think about how to tie your shoelace or drive a car, both very complex processes.

In 'Neuro-Linguistic Programming Vol. 1: The Study of the Structure of Subjective Experience' by Dilts et al, it is asserted that NLP considers conscious awareness an emergent property that only occurs when the intensity of the relevant representational system reaches a certain threshold. If not it just carries on out of conscious awareness.

The one thing that sets (or should set) NLP apart from any other kind of learning process is the process of (formal and deliberate) unconscious instillation.

What is Unconscious Instillation?

It is instilling information in the unconscious mind, right?

Wrong.

It is instilling information at an unconscious level. By which I mean, it sneaks into your mind outside of your conscious awareness and then pops up when you don't expect it (often without realizing you learned it in the first place).

Have you ever found yourself humming a song and have no idea why? There is a good chance that you heard someone else humming it, or heard it on the radio (maybe of a passing car), something that you just didn't register at the time consciously, but that you did pick up unconsciously.

That is unconscious instillation in a nutshell. You pick something up or learn something without being consciously aware that you have learned it.

(It was how, when I was at college, I found I could do my biology homework even though I didn't remember my teacher Phil telling me the stuff...)

Formal "unconscious instillation" utilizes this

natural propensity for our minds to gather information outside of conscious awareness and is a process (or probably, more accurately an 'approach') of embedding learnings and understandings within something else; usually a metaphor and story. It was developed by Richard Bandler after modeling the "teaching tales" of Milton Erickson.

The one thing Bandler and Grinder were clear on when they developed the model of NLP was that people who do things excellently do so unconsciously (without conscious awareness). Just think about something you do on a regular basis that you are proficient, or better at. Think how much conscious focus it requires to carry out that task. The reason that people had difficulty with solving their "problems" (most of us are 'excellent' at continuing to do things we find un-useful!) was that this process was often deeply unconscious. So trying to logically, consciously create change was not overly useful.

And, in fact, if we start to become consciously aware of a process we are excellent at, then we get worse at what we are doing (look at sports people who "choke")!

(The conscious mind just tends to get in the way...)

They developed models, processes and techniques for therapists (and soon, others as well) to observe, map and help change these unconscious processes.

Richard often jokes that the conscious mind is a waste of space (he uses much stronger language than that, if you have seen or heard him talking about it, you will know what I mean) when it comes to learning or activating a skill.

Very quickly they realized that trying to teach these ideas at JUST a conscious level not only took a long, long time but was contradicting what they had discovered so far.

What is Multilevel Communication

There are many confusing and outrageous claims about what multilevel communication actually is. Simply put (and it really is this easy), we process information in two different ways; logically, rationally and methodically, and creatively, imaginatively and narratively.

We tend to consciously process information that is logical, rational and process based, it likes facts and step-by-step methods. It likes demonstrations and tangible processes.

We tend to process metaphorical, creative, and

imaginative ideas and information unconsciously; it likes stories and examples, fairy tales, anecdotes and metaphors.

Multilevel communication is simply combining these two types of learning, but it is about doing it elegantly. Nested Loops gives us an incredibly powerful way of wrapping up the logical information (conscious learning) in the metaphor or story (unconscious learning).

The old left brain/right brain myth (which has been completely discredited by current neuroscience) would talk about the right brain creative side (giving us that urban myth that - since the left field of our perception is processed in the right side of the brain - left handed people are more "creative". Recent studies have shown this is not true) and the left hand side of the brain is more creative.

You may have seen the raft of "pop science" books by people like Malcolm Gladwell, Jonah Lehrer, etc. These books are so clever because they present the information in both the ways our brain likes to process it. They give you the facts and figure, but wrap them up in anecdotes, stories and examples.

This is possibly why they are so popular, they teach people complex ideas without the reader seeming to have to do much work, this makes the reader feel clever!

Like everything, it is a balance, and different people have different tolerances and preferences for fact based and creative learning. Too much story telling and people will start to think you are just telling "irrelevant stories", too much fact based information will send people to sleep.

And since state dictates behavior, above all else you must manage the state of your audience. You need to balance the unconscious and conscious learning depending on the group you are teaching.

I have abandoned examples, stories and anecdotes half way through because the group I have been teaching have clearly become disengaged with the creative approach.

Remember, in NLP the meaning (to the other person) is the response (that you are noticing), if you notice the "wrong" response for the process you are doing, change what you are doing!

PART 3

WHAT NESTED LOOPS AREN'T (BUT YOU NEED TO KNOW BEFORE YOU LEARN NESTED LOOPS)

Now we have covered the basics about what unconscious and conscious learning is and how general multilevel communication works we can start looking at specific approaches that utilize deliberate multilevel communication.

Before we start talking more about what Nested Loops actually are and how to create and use them, we need to spend a bit of time talking about what Nested Loops aren't.

Nested Loops are often confused with two other ways of using stories and metaphor to help create change. They are related to, but not the same as these two different approaches. However, it is important to understand and be proficient in using them before you attempt the more complex Nested Loops structure.

Chaining States

A problem is a state of mind. It is unique, and will exist in its own representational system. In the outcome orientation, you can directionalize the client towards the solution. Once they begin to focus on the Solution State, all you need to do is to get them there. In order to get them there, you need to literally create the steps to enable them to reach the Solution/Desired State:

1. Present/Problem state

2. 1st step towards desired state

3. 2nd step towards desired state

4. Solution/Desired state

The process:

Although above I have given a four-step process, the rule of thumb is to use as few steps as possible.

1. Identify the Present State and Desired State.

2. Set the direction and consider what intermediary states may be useful - what would be a natural and easy step from the previous state? If you are in doubt, it is worth having a conversation with the client and asking them what they think would be useful.

Never be afraid to ask the question. I remember seeing Richard Bandler live once and he invited a delegate on stage for a demonstration. Richard asked him to think of a time when he felt truly motivated and then said to him, "When you think about this time, you see a picture, right?" The delegate said that he did.

Richard turned to the audience and asked, "How did I know he saw a picture?" We all sit there rather dumbly thinking things like, "Maybe he noticed the eye accessing cues, or some other behavioral clue..."

Richard turns to the audience and says, "Because I f--king asked him, that's how I know!"

Never be afraid to ask for clarification, if you presume, or worst, guess, you are projecting your map onto the person you are working with. This goes against the "1st commandment of NLP" that the "map is not the territory". Calibrate to the other persons map and get your own out of the way. You do this by tuning up your sensory acuity and, if in doubt, ask for clarity.

3. Access each state within the client and anchor. This can be done overtly, by asking the client to think of a time when they were in that state, or it can be done via telling a story or anecdote that elicits that state, either conversationally or in trance (or any other way you feel is appropriate to do it). Anchor each step, either overtly or covertly.

4. Go through each step, firing the anchor each time. This can be done in any way you choose from a metaphor to submodality swish (see the step above).

For example:

1. Present State - Certainty about limitations

2. Step 1 - Doubt

3. Step 2 - Curiosity

4. Desired State - Magic(k)al possibilities, freedom and choice.

How many steps do you need?

It is important to understand that this is not a pre-prescribed "technique", but an approach to creating change. You cannot know or plan in advance how many steps you need. See "Don't Be Procrustean" below as well as the details of "How Many Loops?"

Stacking Realities

The first time I saw Richard Bandler on my NLP Practitioner training way back 1999, I didn't really know what to expect. Other than listening to some audiotapes (tapes! Remember them?!) of him I had no clue about what he looked like, his style of delivery or what sort of person he was. So, when he was introduced by Paul McKenna and stalked onto the stage, I was somewhat taken aback. He had long hair tied in a ponytail that was dyed purple, he was wearing big rings, painted fingernails and cowboy boots with flames up the side. When he reached the stage (to the tones of "Voodoo Chile" by Jimi Hendrix!) he didn't introduce himself, he just launched straight into a story about Milton Erickson, I think it went something a bit like this, "The first time I met Milton he looked me straight in the eye with that stare of his and said "I once found a white horse roaming free on the road. I didn't want to let the horse continue to wander around so I caught hold of it's loose reigns and jumped on it's back. I began riding it down the road..."

Now, that is a simple and obvious example of "Stacking Realities". I started talking about my experience (reality 1), of Richard telling a story (reality 2) about how Milton gave him a metaphor for change (reality 3).

But if you dress up the details a bit, make each "reality" rich in detail, use plenty of state based and sensory descriptions and turn them all into shaggy dog tales (tails?), the listener is soon sucked into the flow of the narrative. They lose where you are in the story and just "go with it", once they are in this state of rapt attention you can easily slip in the odd direct or indirect suggestion.

Stacking Realities are first and foremost a way of creating an altered trance state.

Again, the same as Chaining States above and Nested Loops below, it is not a pre-prescribed process, we cannot know beforehand how many realities we will need to stack to create the state/response that we are after.

What's The Difference Between These and Nested Loops?

Let's be quite clear for a moment, these approaches are NOT Nested Loops, no matter what anyone says on YouTube and those "internut" forums!

They are both very useful approaches but have very different applications to Nested Loops. For a start they are linear; they start somewhere and end somewhere else. Nested Loops are (as the name suggests) circular; you end exactly where you started off.

For example, Nested Loops would be useless at getting someone who is stuck to being unstuck. For that you would be better off using the Chaining State approach, if you used Nested Loops, you would just end up taking the client back to where they started (the unwanted state!).

That is not to say that these approaches do not share similarities and some DNA. All three involve the ability to tell effective stories, and metaphors, embed (indirect and direct) suggestions, commands and learnings and create appropriate states.

Chaining States and Stacking Realities are usually taught before Nested Loops as the linear approach means they are easier to grasp and master (I am unsure about other qualifying bodies' syllabuses, but with The Society of NLP, Chaining States and Stacking Realities are taught on the Master Practitioner course, where Nested Loops are not taught until the Trainer Training or Advanced Master Practitioner). You need to start out by getting proficient with the above approaches before you begin to attempt Nested Loops.

One Last Thing - Don't Be Procrustean...

Procrustes was a bandit in ancient Greece (the son of Poseidon, the God of the Sea). He was in the last story of myths of Theseus (the Greek Hero and founder of Athens). Procrustes had a stronghold in the mountains between Athens and Eleusis, where he would invite passers by in for a meal. The food and drink would be drugged and when they passed out, Procrustes would place them on a metal bed. If they were too small for the bed, he would attach them to a rack to stretch them out to make them fit and if they were too big, he would cut bits off...

A *Procrustean bed* has become known as "an arbitrary standard to which exact conformity is forced."

It is used when people try and fit the world to their expectations, rather than the other way round.

Nested Loops are NOT a technique or a process for delivering information in a pre-prescribed manner. This is a fundamental inverse of what Nested Loops are and how they should be used. If you try and turn Nested Loops into a technique or process you are expecting the world to fit your technique not your technique to fit the world. Which means that if things don't go as planned (and lets be honest, things rarely do) you are stuck.

You cannot plan ahead of time what the structure will actually be. You do not know if you will need to chain three or more states, if you can get away with two realities, or if you will need to stack more, or, in the case of Nested Loops, how many loops you will need and where you will need to segue (all this will become clear as we go on).

It is therefore essential that you have the required level of skill in sensory acuity to be able to calibrate to your audience/client and recognize when you have the required response. It is also essential that you have enough flexibility in your behavior to be able to make changes, often on the fly, which is why a rigid "technique" based approach is not useful.

PART 4

WHAT NESTED LOOPS ARE

"Finally!" I hear you cry! We are actually at the part of this book where we discuss how you can go about developing and utilizing Nested Loops...

The Origins of Nested Loops

As Richard explains in his Charisma Enhancement (Trainer) trainings, many of the original models of NLP have been taken from mathematics and computer programming:

"All programming in machines is a mirror image, just like mathematics. Mathematics is THE behavioral science, all of the things that you learn to do, all the NLP things are all mathematical models that I've just zipped off from here and there. I mean, you know, the compulsion blowout is catastrophe theory, it's from how sheet metal and bridges are things. The phobia cure, which blows things out, is from another form of mathematics. I have taken all the mathematics we know that are reliable, because they are mirrors of our neurology, not mirrors of the world. Right, so once we take them back and start doing behavioral things with them, that's why they last as opposed to come out in other symptoms."

Nested Loops is taken from a computer programming terminology, as Richard discusses;

"Nesting Loops is a phenomenon, those of you that have done computer programming will recognize the term, is that what happens is, inside of information processing is that

very often in computers they need to make decisions, so they start what is called a 'For Loop' and what happens is that you end up going and making something you go "something something is equal to X" and then you go X equals and then you have a whole loop that goes around to establish the meaning of what X is. Now sometimes you might, inside of that you may have another For Loop and another For Loop and another For Loop. Some of these things nest pretty deep. What they found out is, is if you violate Nested Loops, what happens is your computer collapses and dies, right, the program explodes and the data is gone. Now this is much akin to the way that when most people will teach, the way they bounce back and forth between ideas, they violate Nested Loops and what happens is is it creates amnesia. And not the kind we want, because amnesia for your problems is one thing, amnesia for the information. Now it's time for us to turn all this around, because what we want to be able to do is get it so that we can put complex patterns inside of people's minds by being able to nest things inside themselves in a way that works. So just when they think they have lost track of what's going on suddenly they begin to understand."

How They Are Structured

Simply put, a Nested Loop is a story within a story. The difference between Nested Loops and Stacking Realities, is that, whereas Stacking Realities is a linear approach, Nested Loops are circular. In Stacking Realities you would start with Story 1 and finish with Story N. In Nested Loops you Start with Story 1 and end with Story 1.

You break each story part way through (other than the last one which you complete in full) and start the next story, until you reach the final loop (how many loops you use depends on the context) then you reverse out, completing the stories in reverse order, something like this:

Start Story 1

/Break/

Start Story 2

/Break/

Tell the Complete Story 3

/Break/

Complete Story 2

/Break/

Complete Story 1

Why Is It a Loop Then, Rather Than Just a Long String of Stories?

Nested Loops work in four ways:

1. They Tap into The Power of Story and Metaphor

We understand the world through story and metaphor. For as long as civilization has been around we have used story and metaphor to describe and explain our experience of reality; Fairytales, Christian parables, the Native American tradition and so on.

As George Lakoff first asserted in "Metaphors We Live By", all thought and communication is metaphorical in nature.

A metaphor, in its broadest definition is "comparing something to something else", or "understanding something in terms of something else".

Even such a simple saying as "I look UP to him", we are using the word "up" to mean **up = good** (think of other phrases when up = good - "I am feeling UP today", "I am UP for it", etc. The converse **down = bad** is also a well-used metaphor).

Because we understand the world through story

and narrative, a well told story will engage and keep the interest and attention of the person you are speaking to much more easily and powerfully than a more cerebral, linear, information based approach.

2. They Prime Our Thinking

Priming is "an implicit memory effect in which exposure to a stimulus influences a response to a later stimulus."

What on earth does that actually mean?

Well, if I showed you an image of the 7 of clubs, 2 dice adding up to 7, a sign saying "deadly sins" and then asked you to think of a number, you are more likely to think of the number 7.

Or, if I showed you the following list of words: feather, fly, nest, egg and then asked you to think of an animal you will probably say "bird".

That is "priming". By giving associated examples it directionalizes your thinking and encourages you to start creating associations for yourself.

Nested Loops can be used to "prime the mind" in the right direction, so when you introduce the learning, the student's mind is already set up to take it in. It therefore makes it easier to learn. There is less "resistance" to the new idea.

3. They Create Expectation and Anticipation

When I was young one my favorite TV shows was The Rocketeer. The re-run was shown in the morning during the school holidays and I would religiously tune in. Each episode always ended a preposterous cliffhanger that was resolved in the first moments of the next episode, but still it kept me coming back every day to see what happened. The idea that leaving a story unfinished, or a loop open, compelled people to return for the next episode has been well used in Hollywood for years!

Our brains hate unfinished material. They keep the story or activity open in our minds and desperately try to close them off. This is why you will find people who have hectic lives tend to be stressed and seem overwhelmed. They constantly interrupt a process and so their mind is trying to sustain all these open and unfinished routines.

As an aside, when Richard was asked to develop a stress management program for executives at a Fortune 500 company in America, the first process he introduced was to get them, at the end of the day, to open and close every drawer or cupboard in the room, close down their computer properly, lift up and put down the telephone, etc. This seemingly odd behavior was designed to make sure that all the physical processes they had started through the day and which had maybe been interrupted would be closed off.

One of the current theories about why we dream suggests that it is our way of trying to sort and close off all the unfinished processes we have been doing during the day. It does this by way of an extended metaphor (see above for the importance of metaphor) that we call "dreams".

The idea that leaving something unfinished will create anticipation is called the **Zeigarnik Effect**. The Zeigarnik effect states that people remember uncompleted or interrupted tasks better than completed tasks.

Psychologist Bluma Zeigarnik first studied the phenomenon after her professor, Gestalt psychologist Kurt Lewin, noticed that a waiter recalled unpaid orders better than paid ones.

The Zeigarnik effect suggests that students who interrupt their studies with unrelated activities, by studying different subjects, etc., will recall material better than students who complete study sessions without a break.

Cicero, the famous Roman orator, philosopher and statesmen used a similar approach in his dialogues. The trick is called *digressio*, you shift from an interesting and engaging story to a secondary story while leaving your original story hanging in mid-air.

Nested Loops use this phenomenon to keep people interested and engaged and encourage them to remember and recall the information more easily.

4. They Wrap Everything Up Neatly and Embed Ideas in Deep

Have you seen the film "Inception"? In it Leonardo DiCaprio's character, Dominick Cobb, is employed to implant an idea deep inside the subconscious mind of the target. He goes "down three levels" in the person's unconscious mind and implants an idea before backing out through each level.

The process of closing the loops off again, rather than the more simple and linear approaches of Stacking Realities or Chaining States means you embed the learnings in deep. You wrap it up in examples, anecdotes and metaphors that help create a more cohesive and complete experience of the learning, allowing the process of **instantiation** to take place more easily.

To understand something we have to make some sort of mental representation of what that means to us. **Instantiation** is the process where we represent a concept by a concrete or tangible example. In learning, instantiation is making that connection between an abstract idea, theory, claim etc. to a real life experience, example or previously understood idea or concept. Like understanding nuclear fission by comparing it to the process of baking bread. Again, this goes back to the principle that we understand everything in terms of something else.

The idea, suggestion or learning is embedded deep down inside the person's mind.

What Can Nested Loops Be Used For? What is the Purpose of Nested Loops?

Before we go on, we must discuss what Nested Loops can be used for. They have developed an almost mythical status of being able to do everything from teaching vast amounts of information in the shortest possible time; to manipulating people into doing what you want; to seducing any woman; to brainwashing people into believing in anything.

The reason for this, as far as I can tell, is because very few people really understand what Nested Loops actually are and (as we have discovered) most people confuse them with other NLP approaches such as Chaining States and Stacking Realities.

In actuality, Nested Loops were developed to,

and are fantastic way of, delivering large quantities of information easily and quickly, whilst keeping the attention of the person or people you are working with. Nested Loops could be used in a formal trance framework if you wished (everything can be adapted and adjusted to suit a desired situation), but really Nested Loops were designed and developed to deliver information in a learning context.

They are an essential skill to master for any teacher or trainer. The goal of Nested Loops is to present material in a way that, when the client goes away, they understand or are capable of doing something without really knowing how they know it or where they learned it!

PART 5

HOW TO DESIGN NESTED LOOPS

Nested Loops require a reasonable amount of effort and focus to learn and perfect. First make sure you are comfortable with some foundational elements of NLP, including:

- The Milton Model.
- Presuppositions.
- Basic rapport skills (including pacing, leading, matching and mirroring).
- Sensory predicates.
- Anchoring (in all representational systems)
- Strategy design and annotation.

When designing your loops you do not need to use the exact order laid down here (although it is always best to define your output first). For example you may already have conscious learning in place and are looking for some loops to wrap around it.

1. Define Your Output

Like everything we do, we need to know where we are going. What decides what loops you are going to use and, most importantly, how will we know when we get the desired response?

The T.O.T.E Model

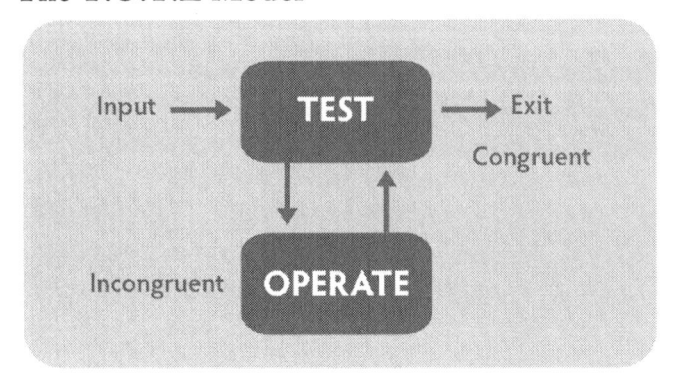

In NLP the T.O.T.E model (developed by Miller, Galanter and Pribram) is the fundamental unit of behavioral analysis and design. We can use the T.O.T.E model to help us determine the relevant output and, most importantly, how you know when you have achieved that output; what is the convincer/"decision point" that lets you know you are "there"?

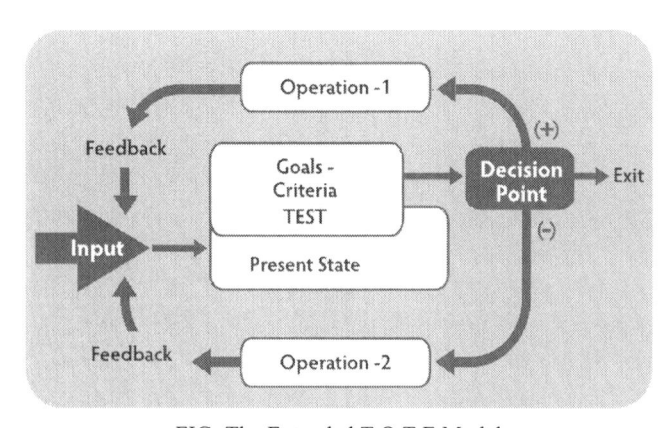

FIG: The Extended T.O.T.E Model

Essential elements for a well-formed T.O.T.E:

1. A well-specified and appropriate Trigger ("What absolutely has to be there for this T.O.T.E to begin?").

2. An Output that is appropriately defined (You can use any outcome design model that is appropriate or that you are comfortable with, from the SMART Goals model to the NLP Well-formed Outcomes Model).

3. A well specified Desired State.

4. A Present State that is appropriately and sufficiently specified.

5. A Test ("Is the Present State the Desired State?") that has adequate criteria for evaluation (the Decision Point - "How do you know?")

6. An Operation Strategy or Sequence that is adequately specified and is efficient and appropriate (check for loops and unnecessary representations).

The T.O.T.E operation follows the following process:

- The Triggering stimulus occurs (an external "anchor").
- The Test ("Is the Present State the Desired State?") is performed.
- If the evaluation is No; then the First Operation sequence is performed.
- On completion of the First Operation, the "Test" is performed again.
- If the evaluation is Yes; then the T.O.T.E is exited.
- If the evaluation is No; then either the First Operation is repeated or a new Operation is performed (a check is in place to evaluate whether the First Operation is appropriate or not).

For example, the volume on the stereo

Trigger - Volume on the stereo

Desired state - "a comfortable volume that I can hear without it being so loud I "can't hear myself think".

Present State - The volume is too loud.

Operation - turn volume down on stereo.

Second Test - Is the volume "a comfortable volume that I can hear with out it being so loud I "can't hear myself think"?

If Yes (the Present State matches the Desired State), then exit the T.O.T.E (the output in this case is the appropriate volume).

If No, repeat the Operation phase - continue to turn the volume down.

This may seem obvious, but once you take into account emotions, personal quirks, prejudiced and interactions with other people, a T.O.T.E can very quickly become muddled and unspecified.

It is essential when designing ANY strategy, not just Nested Loops, to make sure you have a well-formed T.O.T.E.

2. Start With State

NLP is concerned first and foremost with state. Why? Our mental state (emotions, moods feelings, etc.) dictates our behavior. If we are in a bad state, we tend to make bad decisions and "do" inappropriate behaviors. Think what state would be appropriate in the context in which you are in. We will see how to tell "state eliciting" stories in a little while.

3. Choose an Appropriate "Conscious Learning"

What are you going to place in the middle of the loop? This could be a story as an explicit example, it could be step-by-step process, it could be a practical exercise. It could be all three! Or something else entirely.

How to instill the conscious learning

You have several choices available to you to "instill' (teach) the conscious part of the learning:

- You can break the final story in the loop and then teach the learning as an overt and explicit process.

- You can get the delegates to do a practical exercise.

- You can use the final story in the loop as an explicit example of the learning and break the story down chunk by chunk.

- You can use a "Socratic Learning" strategy - asking questions to help the students work it out for themselves. This journey of self-discovery can be one of the most powerful learning methods; the student feels empowered and emboldened by their ability to "work it out". If you have used your loops to prime appropriately, the students should know, or be able to instantiate (generate and extrapolate from previous knowledge) the answers without consciously knowing where or how they did it.

Again, there is no "right" way to teach the conscious learning, it depends on the context which you are in and your available options. Experiment with different approaches and see what works for you.

4. Decide How Many Stories You Need

Remember, this is an approach not a technique, but you do need to have in mind different ideas for stories and examples, preferably with some in "reserve" in case you are not getting the response that you want.

You will need different stories for different contexts - using therapy based examples within a corporate training (unless well framed and contextualized) may not be as well received and useful as using corporate based examples.

There is also no harm, when first learning Nested Loops, to have a more "process based" approach. Planning and scripting out your stories in more detail, as well as having a rough idea where and how to segue into the next story. We will talk more about that in a little while.

6. Choose What Stories To Tell

This does depend a lot on what you are trying to teach or instill.

I tend to open my "Frame Loop", with a specific example or anecdote relating to the subject or topic I am teaching, but you don't need to do that, you can start with an unrelated story to elicit the appropriate state.

Broadly there are two types of stories or metaphor:

Isomorphic Metaphor
Isomorphism can be defined as "Being of identical or similar form, shape, or structure." What this means in the context of a story is you talk about a similar experience or example that directly relates to the subject you are teaching.

It may work something like this:

"So, you want to learn to spell better? I had a friend who couldn't spell very well, so he decided to do something about it, this is what he did..."

Homomorphic Metaphor

Homomorphic is defined as "Similarity of external form or appearance but not of structure or origin." A Homomorphic metaphor is a story, example or metaphor that elicits the appropriate state, the content of the story my have no (obvious) relevance to the topic.

If you have decided that curiosity would be a useful state to elicit from your audience, you tell a story about being curious, it may or may not be relevant in content to the subject you are teaching.

When used elegantly, homomorphic metaphors are incredibly powerful. People who miss this subtlety are often the ones who accuse Richard Bandler of telling "irrelevant stories". He is using homomorphic metaphor to elicit the appropriate state.

I often use homomorphic metaphor within my training loops to break state and "refresh" the delegates. If I notice that the group is slipping from the state I want or need during a prolonged or complex Training Frame, I will "interrupt myself" and tell an amusing story, anecdote or joke. I will usually make sure I place a humorous anchor in the group early on, so that I can also fire off that anchor, just to make sure...

Finding Stories to Use: Your "Story Book"

You have a variety of options to what stories you can tell; truism, parables, quotes, your own or other people's experiences that have been smoothed and shaped into a polished anecdote, metaphors, fairy stories, fables, short pithy jokes or long rambling shaggy dog stories. It really does all depend on the context and the response that you want.

I highly suggest you start collecting stories, from any and all sources. I have a vast bookshelf full of stores from Grimm's fairy tales, to Baron Münchhausen, to Shakespeare.

I am never afraid to reference the person I heard the story from. I think, personally, it is a type of fraud to lay claim to a story that isn't yours and, in my experience, it makes little difference to the power of the story if you reference the person you heard it from. In some cases, this may actually give you more credibility, as you appear well researched.

How to Tell Stories

Telling stories is a skill. There is a fine line between being a loquacious, charismatic raconteur and thundering bore. The same story, told by two different people can come across torturously dull or thrillingly engaging.

The first thing you need to do to get good at story telling is to love communicating by story telling. Not only you telling stories, but you hearing them too (if you don't like being told a good story then it is doubtful you will be able to tell one).

This book is not here as a story telling manual, but since being able to tell a good tale is an important skill when weaving your Nested Loops, here are a few tips to become a more elegant and engaging storyteller:

1. **Remember the NLP presupposition that the "meaning of communication is the response that you get."** It is not about what you think you are saying but about what your listener thinks you are saying that is important. Remember that they will interpret your communication through their own filters and criteria, which may or may not correlate with your own. You may think your story is incredible and amazing, but you don't count in this situation. It is what your audience thinks that counts! Make the story you are telling relevant to the audience and make sure you are telling it for the right reasons (I have seen many people use stories just to brag...).

2. **Pay attention.** To do this you need to get out of your own head and calibrate to the group. It is one of the reasons why you have to prepare so fully; you don't want to be inside your head thinking about what you are going to say next, you want to be outside, paying attention to the group you are telling the story to.

3. **Don't be afraid to stop.** If you are not getting the response that you want, don't be afraid to stop and change subject or story. Being able to elegantly switch stories is one of the main ingredients to Nested Loops, so it is worth taking the time to master it.

4. **Get in state.** A simple rule is "if you want someone to do something, you do it first", also known as "leading" in rapport building. It is much easier to get the group to go into a state if you get into that state first.

5. **Use lots of sensory rich language.** We understand the world through our five senses, so when we are describing that world to other people, you need to use sensory based language to powerfully enrich the story.

6. **Use your body.** If appropriate, use plenty of body language, gestures and moving around (but remember, sometimes the most powerful states can be produced by standing totally still). A famous study by Albert Mehrabian suggested that 55% of the meaning we take from communication (whether we like it, agree with it or find it congruent) is through body language.

7. **Check your tone (and the speed and rate you speak).** A great story can be ruined if you talk in a dull monotone or nasally tone. Record yourself speaking and see how you sound. Take some voice coaching lessons (or get some off the internet) if you are not happy with the sound of your voice. Be careful of the speed and rate that you speak. Vary the speed depending on the state but don't talk too fast as it will sound like you are rushing it (and may be unclear).

This, of course, is not a book on modeling and to go into the modeling process here would be going off topic. But it would be to helpful to brush up on your modeling skills and model storytellers you find particularly engaging. I have, in my time, modeled attributes of Billy Connolly, Eddie Izzard, Stephen Fry and Richard Bandler (obviously!), to name a few.

Read and listen to great storytellers, stand up comedians and speechmakers (YouTube is one of the greatest resources available for this sort of thing! When I first started out YouTube didn't exist and I had to be very creative in how I found and modeled good storytellers - buying and renting videos and books from the library was my usual approach).

Start introducing stories into your training courses or one-to-one sessions or when you are talking to people (not as loops to begin with, but just as short examples or anecdotes).

How Long Should Your Stories Be?

As the old saying goes, "how long is a piece of string?" It all depends on your audience, context and time available. Never rush your stories, you will appear apologetic and unsure, but do not ramble either. You need to practice them to find just the right length. To paraphrase Einstein, a story, anecdote or metaphor should be "as long as needed and no longer". You have to judge the target of the story and the purpose of that story. I have told stories on training courses that have been a minute long; a comical quip to change state that is a sentence; an anecdote to link topics, or as an introductory story to get people relaxed, focused or motivated that has lasted five minutes.

Some stories I tell can last half an hour or more if they are illustrating a teaching point, or I am presenting the conscious learning within the story.

3. Decide on the Structure

This will often be dictated by the context in which you are using the Nested Loops, whether it is a one hour session or a multi-day training. We will talk more about more advanced and complex looping structures a little later on, for now here is the simplest looping method.

How to Structure Your Loops

Remember Nested Loops are not a technique, it is not a pre-prescribed process. Nested Loops are a way of presenting information in way that makes it more easily "digestible", but it does tend to follow a commonly recognizable structure:

Take what you want to teach and think of three to five stories that are relevant to what you are teaching. Make them a mix of Homomorphic (creating the appropriate state) and Isomorphic (containing knowledge, process, skills or suggestions) metaphors:

START STORY 1

/BREAK and SEGUE TO…

START STORY 2

/BREAK and SEGUE TO…

START STORY 3

/BREAK and SEGUE TO…

INSTALL CONSCIOUS LEARNING, OR UTILISE STORY 3 TO GIVE LEARNING.

FINISH STORY 3

/BREAK and SEGUE TO…

FINISH STORY 2

/BREAK and SEGUE TO…

FINISH STORY 1

So, say you are going to teach a new skill, like the

NLP spelling strategy, it could go something like this:

STORY 1: A brief history of the spelling strategy, including stories Richard Bandler has told about how he developed the strategy and used it to teach it to school children (this has elements of "Stacking Realities" to it so it is also a good way of getting attention). This is an **isomorphic metaphor**.

STORY 2: A **homomorphic metaphor** about something I found difficult when learning it, but now find easy and simple to do (learning to drive a car for example) to overcome any limiting beliefs about their ability to learn.

STORY 3: How I personally used the spelling strategy to overcome my dyslexia. This is **both an isomorphic metaphor** - giving an example of where the strategy was used - **and a homomorphic metaphor**, creating the belief that this is a powerful strategy that will work.

CONSCIOUS LEARNING: The actual Spelling Strategy, including a demonstration and practical exercise where they go of and instill it in each other. I could tell this as part of story 3, using my experience to frame the process, jumping backward and forwards between the story and the conscious learning.

When and How to Segue

Remember, Nested Loops are not a "technique" they are a principle, a method, a heuristic (rule of thumb) to help get important and complicated information into people's heads and make it stick.

Therefore, like all good methodology, it must be dynamic.

If you pre-plan all your loops and when to break each story, you are turning the approach into a process or technique. You are not interacting, or responding to feedback from the people you are working with. You are simply doing Nested Loops **at** people. Which may, or may not, get the response and results that you want.

You segue (a musical term meaning "move without interruption"), change story, and start a new loop **when you get the response that you want**. This could occur after the first sentence, it could occur almost all of the way through the anecdote or story. Sometimes you may need to loop back to intensify or even, if you are not getting the desired response, abandon that anecdote altogether and use a "backup story". It is important to have the necessary behavioral flexibility to be able to adapt your Nested Loops on the fly to suit your audience and calibrate to the relevant feedback.

There may seem to be a really neat place in your story that you think you can segue to the next loop. The problem with this is, if you have not got the audience the appropriate response for that loop, breaking there will be totally counter productive.

A Note On Encouraging Feedback

It is essential, therefore, to calibrate to your audience; to make sure you are getting the appropriate response. This means, first and foremost, you need to tune up your senses and get out of your head and pay attention to the people you are working with. So many people I see deliver trainings or one-to-one work are so busy concentrating on their state and what they are going to say and do next (some to the extent they are simply reading a script!) that they miss all the feedback cues.

Many people I work with are often afraid to ask for feedback, they somehow think they need to be able to notice it all by themselves, and asking for feedback is somehow a sign of failure or weakness. This is simply not the case, it is very helpful to explicitly create a feedback mechanism. You may, if you have seen Richard Bandler train, notice that he often says (nods his head) "This means yes," (Shakes his head), "This means no. We will be using them all week." This creates a feedback mechanism that you can use simply by asking "Does that make sense?" or some other appropriate question.

A Note On Looping Back

Once you have completed the "front end" of your loop and want to start cycling back, at an unconscious level you want to signal to the group that you are now closing things up.

So, it can be helpful to install some sort of anchor for each loop, this could be spatial (where you stand or sit), tonal (changing your voice, the speed and rate you speak), gestural (changing gross body language) or any other way you like. I tend to use a mixture, depending on what I am teaching and how many loops I am using. Anchors are also useful for you - they can trigger the loop off in your mind.

A Beginners Loop

Start simply. Don't dive straight into a five-loop process or a complicated multi-loop structure. Once you are comfortable just telling simple stories and anecdotes completely, start with two stories and wrap the second one up in the first one:

Start Story 1

/Break and segue to…

Tell Story 2 in its entirety

/Segue to...

Complete Story 1

Michael Breen, the NLP Master Trainer, often says, "If you need a script to tell you what to say and you are not an actor, you are an idiot." He has a point! His somewhat blunt statement is, of course, deliberately controversial. He says it to remind us not to become Procrustean about our approach.

However, saying that, when you are starting out, scripting out your stories, segues and loops is an important step in mastering Nested Loops. I remember, when I very first got into NLP, I bought a block of school notebooks from my local stationers and would spend hours writing out examples of all the language patterns I had learned and scripts using all those language patterns. I would record them into a Dictaphone and listen back to see how it sounded. I still do this to this day.

There is no shortcut. You have to put in the hours (In his book Outliers, Malcolm Gladwell suggests you need to spend 10,000 hours on a subject or skill before you master it. This is not an exact figure, much in the same way that the Ancient Taoists would refer to 1001 things meaning lots and lots, the '10,000 hours' illustrates that it takes a lot of time and effort to master a skill).

After designing and writing them out in full, very quickly you will be able develop your own shorthand for designing your loops.

Nowadays, when designing a new training course, I don't need to fully map and script it out, I use a similar strategy to Billy Connolly (the famous Scottish stand up comedian); I write down a key word or phrase to trigger the loop that I am going use and the order of the stories, examples or practical demonstrations in that loop. I will define the learning outcome for the course, chunk it down to the required frames and bullet point out each story or anecdote and "conscious learning" for each frame.

I developed this idea after watching Billy Connolly's "World Tour of England, Ireland and Wales" DVD, in one episode he holds a tattered, tea stained piece of paper up to the camera, with a scrawl of words listed on it and says something like, "These are my notes for tonight."

If those are his "notes", that he uses to keep track

whilst weaving his magically entertaining loops on stage, then it is good enough for my training design (of course, mine are little more detailed than his!).

PART 6

GOING DEEPER – MULTIPLE LOOPS

Once you have started to get comfortable with a simple singular looping structure of three to five stories you can start playing with the format to create different results depending on the context.

A simple three to five story looping structure is absolutely fine if you are teaching one thing, but what happens on a multi-day training, or a course covering more than one topic, subject or piece of information?

Loops Within Loops

When designing longer, more complex courses you will find you need more than one set of Nested Loops. You will need to break down what you want to get across into manageable chunks.

You can loop each topic and also create an overarching set of loops for the whole course, each day, etc., depending on what suits your needs.

Remember this is as much an art as it is a science, there is no fixed or 'right' way to do Nested Loops (as long as you follow the core methodology), so now you understand the basic principles you can play with them to create a way that works best for you and the results you want to achieve.

With a multi-day training you will tend to want to

break down the course into three broad looping structures:

1. Training Loops

This is the largest level of information chunk, in this loop you will spend time framing the overarching aims and themes of the training course and eliciting and anchoring appropriate states at this important high level. You may reference what you are going to do in each day and even each frame, to forward pace.

A HINT: You can use the Training Loop to scale the content of the training. By which I mean this: Chunking up is about deciding what to leave out. In this case the more detailed information and exercises. So if you want to do a shorter version of the workshop use the Training Loop as the Frame Loop.

Backtracking and Future Pacing

The old adage about teaching is "say what you are going to say, say it and then say that you have said it."

Repetition is an essential part of learning. What we do over and over again we get better at (even if it is a behavior that is not particularly useful!). Nested Loops, by their very nature, allow us to structure our presentations, workshops and training courses in a way that naturally and elegantly backtracks and forward paces the information presented.

Backtracking is repeating the same information, often in different ways and then using that to launch into a new subject or extend and add more detail to the previous subject. It creates a flow and association between topics or subjects.

Future Pacing is a form of mental rehearsal. Our brain is not very good at telling the difference between imagination and reality (because, as far as our neurology is concerned, everything happens on the "inside"). If you explain to someone what they are going to do later on, they have to make some sort of mental representation of (imagining themselves) doing it for it to make sense to them. This mental rehearsal helps create the associations and strategies for actually doing it.

2. Daily Loops

A Daily Loop is a way of framing and tying together everything you are going to teach that day. A typical day's training will consist of more than one Frame Loop (if not, you don't need the Daily Loop). These Training Frames may or may not be related. A Daily Loop will allow you to Forward Pace and Backtrack on what you have covered to package it all up neatly, create associations and encourage instantiation.

3. Frame or Chunk Loops

The most detailed chunk of your training will be a specific Training Frame or Training Chunk (which phrase you use tends to be up to the individual trainer. For example, Michael Breen tends to use the phrase "Training Frame", Christina Hall tends to use "Training Chunk").

A Training Frame or Chunk is how you break down a larger training into smaller subject based modules. Some trainers base their frames or chunks around a time based approach, where a frame will be approximately an hour to an hour and a half. I prefer to build my frame around subjects, so frames can be anything from half an hour to a whole day depending on the subject covered. It is up to you which you prefer and what is appropriate to the context you are presenting.

Multiple Loop Example Layout

An example of a 2-day workshop utilizing Nested Loops could look something like this:

NESTED LOOPS DEMYSTIFIED

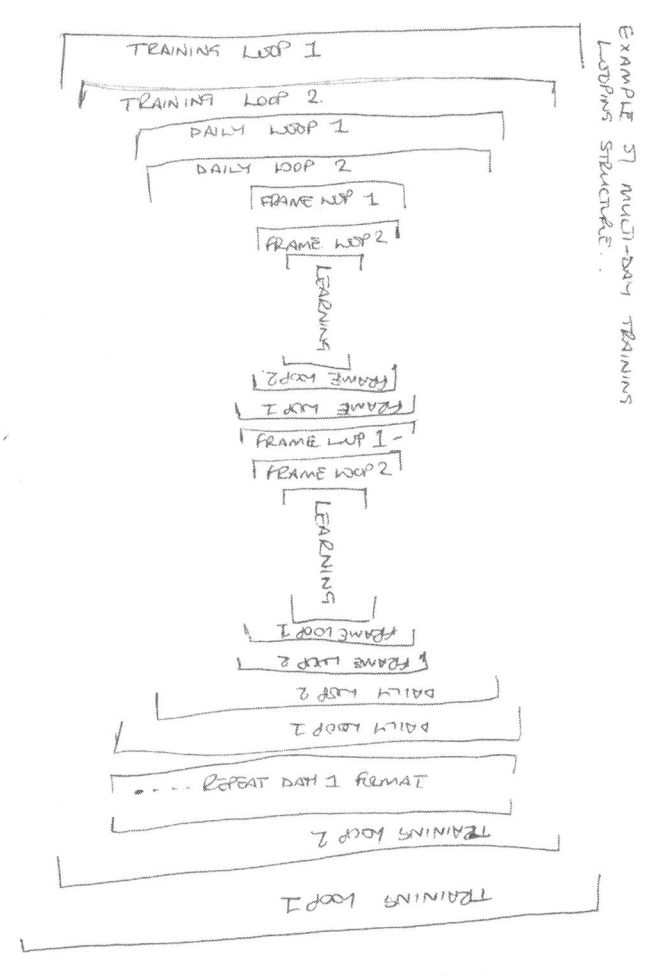

FIG: Example of Multi-day Training Looping Structure

PART 7

GOING EVEN DEEPER - GETTING CREATIVE

Nested Loops are an art and you are an artist. Words are your brushes, canvas and paints...

And like any good artist, you need to learn where you can break with convention, stamp your mark on what you are doing and create bold new works and movements.

So far I have laid out the core principles and methodology of creating Nested Loops and how to apply that to several different structures and contexts.

Once you feel comfortable with that you will learn which of these "rules" you can bend and which rules you can "break"...

None-Story Loops

You don't have to just use stories to create your loops. They are just the most common approach. As I have said all along, Nested Loops are not a technique or a process, there is no one right way to do them. With a little ingenuity and creativity you can use all sorts of things as loops.

You could use practical exercises and demonstrations as loops, either on their own or in conjunction with stories.

I have used a practical exercise loop when

teaching the Presupposition Language Patterns.

The opening exercise is to simply listen to their training partner talk briefly about a subject and notice what presuppositions are being used - they will not have the titles at the stage, the goal is to notice what they think is being presupposed in the conversation; what has to be there for their statements to make sense. I then go through a process (using some more practical exercises, examples and stories as loops) of teaching the presuppositions and then close off the first loop by getting them to redo the exercise and see how many more presuppositions they notice. This is a great "convincer" as they realize how much was going on, but they just hadn't noticed it yet...

Breaking Stories Into More Than Two Parts Per Loop

So far we have mainly discussed a very simple looping structure where you break the story in 2, telling half on the "way in" and half on the "way back out". However, with practice you can start experimenting with breaking the story up into more than two parts. For example:

Story Part 1

/Break/

Conscious learning Part 1

/Break/

Story Part 2

/Break/

Conscious learning Part 2

/Break/

Rinse and repeat, until finished.

We mentioned this in the early section where we discussed Cicero's trick of *digressio*, where you break from an interesting and engaging story to a secondary story/conscious learning while leaving your original story hanging in mid-air.

It is something I have seen Michael Breen do very effectively, sometimes he will leave the story hanging and not actually finish it, leaving the loop open...

HINT: When running multi-day training courses you may want to return to the Training Loop or

Daily Loop several times throughout the course to Backtrack and Future Pace.

Leaving Some Loops Open

As we have discovered, our mind hates unfinished business. Because of this it can be a good idea to leave some loops open after a training course or a session. This means the delegate will continue to process, contemplate and consider what they have learned a long time after the official training has finished. You could leave some loops open in a way that encourages the delegates to close them for themselves, maybe by giving half an example, anecdote or truism and dropping a few hints about how they can go about closing it off for themselves. This process of guided self-discovery can be immensely empowering for the delegate.

PART 8

WHAT NEXT?

Well, that is it. We have discusses Nested Loops in great detail.

We have gone through some of the essential core concepts that are often very misunderstood, but that you need to know before attempting Nested Loops.

We have talked about what Nested Loops aren't and covered two very powerful NLP approaches that, in their own right, can create exceptional results when used in the right context (but are not Nested Loops). I highly recommend you get comfortable with these before even attempting Nested Loops.

We have talked about some of the reasons why Nested Loops work. Although not essential, understanding some of the conceptual framework that sits behind the Nested Loops approach can be very useful.

It is much like listening to a piece of music. A newcomer, who knows nothing about the composition can appreciate it, it can have an emotional impact. But by learning a little about how music is composed and the skill involved (even if they never intend to compose or play music themselves) will deepen their appreciation and intensify the emotional connection.

If I had dived straight in and taught you how to do Nested Loops without giving you some of the conceptual framework as to how the approach works, you may have had a basic, workman like and perfunctory ability to create Nested Loops, but would not have had the deeper appreciation that will allow you to develop your own artistic and creative uses of the approach. Understanding the underlying concepts allows you to more quickly learn which rules you can bend and which rules you can break.

And finally we have discussed how you can create your own loops, how to wrap loops within loops and how to break them up. You have learned a little about what to use in your loops and where you can use stories, examples and exercises to create Backtracking and Forward Pacing.

I hope you have found this book a useful introduction, primer and guide to Nested Loops. My goal was to undo much of the mysticism and mythology that surrounds this approach and give you, as much as I could, a clear and concise process for starting to develop your own loops.

Practice, Practice, Practice

However, just reading this book is not enough, you now need to practice, practice, practice.

Remember this is starter guide, to get you going. There are many more things you can do to improve your skill and subtlety with this art. Here is a suggested route to getting proficient at Nested Loops. This is only a suggestion, so adjust according to your level of ability and interests:

1. Make sure you are comfortable and confident about using the foundation NLP methodology. The deeper and stronger your foundation, the higher and stronger you can go. Everyone, so far without exception, that I have met who is exquisite with NLP has put in the long, long hours of practicing the basics.

2. Start modeling other people and learn from them:
    - Read lots of stories.
    - Listen and watch great storytellers, presenters, actors and speechmakers. The Internet is a fantastic resource for this, with sites like YouTube full of clips you can watch.
    - Map, transcribe and model how other people use Nested Loops. Standup comedians such as Billy Connolly use a looping structure within their routines. But for pure NLP Nested Loops, used the way they were designed and created to be used, you

are best to watch, listen to and transcribe Richard Bandler. There is a wealth of Richard Bandler products available as well as clips on YouTube, etc. If you can, transcribe sections of his talks and note where, and how, he elegantly segues from one loop/story to the next.

3. Practice story telling; tell stories everywhere you can. But do it with a purpose and make sure you have some way of tracking the results. It is all well and good telling stories all day long, but if all you are doing with them is boring people stupid you are not really getting the appropriate outcome. So, when telling stories, make sure you have a reason for doing so and you are doing it in an appropriate way in an appropriate place. Introduce simple stories and examples into your training courses and workshops.

4. Start collecting stories, literally keep a "story book" and jot ideas down for stories; experiences you have had, other peoples stories and experiences, anecdotes, truisms, fables, etc. Make sure you make a note of what the story could be used for. Are they to create a particular state? Give a useful learning? Both?

5. Start using stories to stack realities and create chains of states.

6. When you are comfortable with telling stories and using them to stack realities and chain states, start with a basic loop. Just loop one story within another: At this stage you will probably want to script and plot it out in much more detail than you will need to when you have become proficient.

7. Now you can start doing simple Frame Loops. During a training you are comfortable with, you can redesign a section, chunk or frame with a simple Nested Loops structure. Do one frame at a time; this gives you the opportunity to get comfortable with the process before diving into a fully redesigned training.

8. Finally you can start doing the full Monty; introduce loops within loops, breaking loops into more than one part and figuring out your own personal Nested Loops style. Remember: Everyone is different, we all have different personalities and communication styles, so even though it is very useful to model and map other people using Nested Loops, do not simply

copy or mimic the surface structure of their approach. Develop your own unique way of presenting.

How long you spend on each stage depends on your confidence and ability and the amount of time you can spend practicing. Don't rush through each step, but don't hang around for too long either, you need to challenge yourself.

To get a bonus chapter of this book, with additional training design resources, including a training design template detailed notes and a worked example please visit:

www.nlpdemystified.com/nestedloopsbonus

Don't take my word for it, I make no claims to be "The Nested Loops Guru", I am not the best at developing, creating and weaving them, I am not the world authority on Nested Loops. I encourage you to go and check everything I have told you (and don't just look at Wikipedia...).

A Final Note

I thought about writing this whole book as a series of Nested Loops, but as we have discovered, you cannot plan loops in that way, as where to break the loop is dependent on the audience or person we are speaking to and the state they are in. We cannot predetermine the breaks, so trying to write this book in the Nested Loop form would just contradict what I have spoken about. Although the keener student may notice where I have slipped some in here and there.

But anyway, I have strayed somewhat from telling you about that eventful evening in Birmingham, when I first heard Richard Bandler...

To get a bonus chapter of this book, with additional training design resources, including a training design template detailed notes and a worked example please visit:

www.nlpdemystified.com/nestedloopsbonus

Made in the USA
Charleston, SC
15 April 2014